BUGGY FRIENDLY WALKS

in The Than

Catharine Gregory

COUNTRYSIDE BOOKS
NEWBURY BERKSHIRE

First published 2012
© Catharine Gregory 2012

COUNTRYSIDE BOOKS
3 Catherine Road
Newbury, Berkshire

To view our complete range of books,
please visit us at
www.countrysidebooks.co.uk

ISBN 978 1 84674 292 7

Designed by Peter Davies, Nautilus Design
Produced through MRM Associates Ltd., Reading
Printed by Information Press, Oxford

Contents

@@

Contents

Introduction

At some point after having a baby, most new mums get to a stage where they would quite like to start exercising again. What better way than to get outdoors with your baby in a stroller, perhaps team up with some other mums and power walk your way back to fitness and into your old jeans. But where can you go? What if your baby needs changing or feeding? Will the park be too muddy or the road too busy?

Before I had a baby, I knew lots of local walks but I soon found that none of them were at all suitable for buggies. I tried using a baby sling but my little boy soon became too heavy for long walks and there was nowhere to put him if I went to a café. It became clear that there were lots of other mums like me, who wanted to go for a nice walk but didn't know where to start. So, I decided to investigate local footpaths and bridleways for their buggy-friendliness.

What is a buggy-friendly walk?

I have created a series of lovely country walks in the Thames Valley that can be enjoyed by anybody but also happen to be suitable for buggies. I have also included information on cafés and pubs and baby-changing facilities. The walks are designed for you, the mum (or the dad or the grandparent) so that you can enjoy a good walk and have the benefits of exercise without having to commit yourself to regular classes or find childcare.

These walks have been tested on a variety of prams and strollers, most of which are not specifically designed as 'outdoorsy'. Paths are not all tarmac so you should expect some bumpiness and some mud. However, I have done my best to avoid:

- Stiles
- Rutted paths
- Flights of steps
- Small kissing-gates
- Very narrow paths
- Busy roads (unless they have pavements)
- And other obstacles that make walking with a buggy impossible.

I have also given a terrain guide for each walk. Some paths are a breeze during a hot summer, only to turn into a quagmire during a wet winter so do be careful if doing a walk after a prolonged bout of rain. Where possible, I have given 'winter' options to enable you to avoid certain paths in bad weather.

Buggy Friendly Walks in The Thames Valley

Of course some winters are dry while summers can be wet so please take a look at how soft the ground is before attempting a 'summer' route.

Facilities

Clearly, if you have a small child or baby, then toilets and baby-changing facilities will be important and I have listed all that I could find. I have also tried to note all the possible places to buy refreshments en route, which I know from experience will be particularly important to breast-feeding mothers!

How far?

Remember that walking with a buggy is an all-over body workout and far more strenuous than walking without a buggy so be careful not to be too ambitious in either distance or time expectations. Two miles an hour is good going on a non-tarmac path but you should manage three miles an hour on tarmac. Where possible, I have given shortcuts to use as escape routes if you or your little one want to get back to the car.

Health guidelines suggest you should wait until six weeks after giving birth before you take part in strenuous exercise. Not all the walks in this book are strenuous but some are, so do be careful in those first few weeks and be prepared to turn around if you are finding it difficult. If you have had a caesarean section, then you may need to wait longer and do make sure that your doctor has given you the all-clear to start exercising.

Did you know that brisk walking with a stroller burns approximately 260 calories per hour, 80 calories more than without the stroller?

Equipment

This is common sense really and not so different from what you might take with you when walking to the shops or going on a picnic but do remember – depending on the season:

- Blankets and raincover for buggy
- Waterproof jacket for you (umbrellas are too much hard work when pushing a pram)
- Sunhat and suncream for you and baby
- Waterproof map cover (for this book)
- Bottle of water and snacks
- Nappy bag etc for your little one.

You do not need a specific pram or buggy, as these walks are designed to suit most. However, if you are in any doubt as to the sturdiness of your vehicle, then I suggest starting on one of the easier all-year-round walks such as Holyport, Goring or Dinton Pastures.

Health & Safety

Please remember to strap your baby into the buggy! When you stop somewhere, do use the brake, as buggies can start rolling down the slightest of inclines. If you are going up or down a slope, try to face it head-on, particularly if you have a three-wheeled buggy as these can become unstable at an angle.

Do make sure that you carry water and whatever sustenance your baby requires. Once babies are on solids, baby snacks such as biscuits or breadsticks can be a lifesaver if your baby starts crying, and will give you an extra half hour to get back to the car or find somewhere where you can sit down and feed your baby properly.

Most modern buggies have puncture-proof wheels but some

of the all-terrain pushchairs are susceptible to punctures so you may want to carry a repair kit or spare wheel if yours is one of those.

If it is muddy and you are finding the walk hard-going, do check that you haven't accumulated a load of mud in your wheel arches, as that really does make it harder to push the buggy. If you have, a poke with a stick should sort things out.

Thanks

Finally, I would like to say a huge 'thank you' to all my friends from Birthmatters, who have helped test the walks, as well as the pubs and teashops; to my friend Caroline for devising the Cookham walk; and many thanks to Tony Jones for taking all the buggy photographs; and to my family for coming on so many of the walks.

Catharine Gregory

PUBLISHER'S NOTE

We hope that you obtain considerable enjoyment from this book; great care has been taken in its preparation. Although at the time of publication all routes followed public rights of way or permitted paths, diversion orders can be made and permissions withdrawn.

We cannot, of course, be held responsible for such diversion orders and any inaccuracies in the text which result from these or any other changes to the routes nor any damage which might result from walkers trespassing on private property. We are anxious though that all details covering the walks are kept up to date and would therefore welcome information from readers which would be relevant to future editions.

The simple sketch maps that accompany the walks in this book are based on notes made by the author whilst checking out the routes on the ground. They are designed to show you how to reach the start, to point out the main features of the overall circuit and they contain a progression of numbers that relate to the paragraphs of the text.

However, for the benefit of a proper map, we do recommend that you purchase the relevant Ordnance Survey sheet covering your walk. The Ordnance Survey maps are widely available, especially through booksellers and local newsagents.

Don't know where to start? Here are my ideas of walks that are good for:

All the family: Burnham Beeches (great woods for children to play in), Maidensgrove Common (great for running around, kite-flying), California Country Park (fabulous playground and paddling pool)

Running: Windsor Great Park, Dorney Lake and Two Rivers, Dinton Pastures

First proper walk after giving birth: Holyport, Goring

The more adventurous: Shiplake, Checkendon and Stoke Row

Picnic: Windsor Great Park (by the Copper Horse statue), Hambleden (by the river), Maidensgrove Common (on the common, with views over the Chilterns)

Afternoon tea: Windsor Great Park (at Savill Garden café), Goring (Pierreponts Café)

Family-friendly pub lunch: Maidenhead Thicket, Highmoor, Mapledurham (in fact, almost all of the walks have lovely pubs en route but do check opening hours and whether booking is recommended)

AREA MAP SHOWING THE LOCATIONS OF THE WALKS

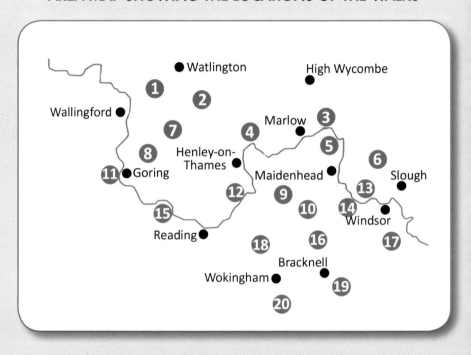

Ewelme

Glorious Chiltern views

Ewelme, viewed from across the fields.

The historic village of Ewelme is a delight to explore. The longer walk gives you some lovely country air and great Chiltern views, passing fields edged with poppies and thistles, but it is one of the more strenuous walks in this book and not for the faint-hearted. The short walk gives you all the delights of the village and more besides, including the lovely Cow Common.

Buggy Friendly Walks in The Thames Valley

1

Distance: 5 miles; short option: 3 miles.
Time: 2½ hours, plus stopping time for the full route; short option: 1½ hours.
Terrain: Lanes, footpaths and bridleways. The long walk includes some rougher paths and is suitable in summer only. The short walk should be do-able most of the year, except after prolonged periods of rainfall, as long as you don't mind a bit of mud.
Start/Parking: The free public car park by the recreation ground on Ewelme High Street. Take the A4074 towards Wallingford and, at the roundabout with the A4130, follow the signs towards Ewelme. On entering the village, turn right along the High Street and look for the car park ahead, next to the sports ground. OS map: Explorer 171 Chiltern Hills West; GR SU646912.
Refreshments: The Shepherd's Hut pub in Ewelme has highchairs and a garden with a play area. ✆ 01491 836636. Ewelme Store sells ice-creams and light refreshments, and has a couple of tables inside and out.
Suggested picnic spot: Cow Common, near the start of the walk.

The Walk

❶ From the car park, head down the grassy slope to the left of the cricket pitch towards the large kissing-gate. Go through the gate and straight ahead through Cow Common, along an obvious grassy track. At the trees, go through a large kissing-gate and emerge onto a lane.

❷ At the lane, either (short route) turn right along the lane for 500 metres and then turn right along a bridleway, signposted Chiltern Way. Skip to point 4. Or (long route) turn

left along the lane and at a junction turn right along a bridleway towards Down Farm. Pass the farm and continue along the track. At a cross-tracks turn right along a bridleway (chalky track).

❸ After ½ mile, reach cross-tracks and turn right, slightly uphill. After 400 metres, the path forks and you head left but soon turn right (along the Chiltern Way) at the next junction and continue in this direction for about ½ mile, to reach a lane. Turn right along the lane and then immediately turn left along a bridleway, signposted Chiltern Way.

View from the almshouses.

continue down the lane into the village.

5 Turn left along the High Street. After passing the village duck pond, turn right up Parsons Lane. Ewelme Store is on your left. As the lane bears right, look out for Chaucer Court (cul-de-sac) on your left. Turn left here and turn left again along a gravel path. Skirt round to the left of 'The Hyde' to continue along a bridleway in the same direction for 600 metres to reach a lane and turn left. You soon reach the Shepherd's Hut pub on your left.

6 Take the next left into the High Street. Notice the watercress beds on your right.

4 (The **short route** rejoins here.) The bridleway is a grassy path on the left-hand edge of a field and continues along a path between fences with a quarry on your left. At the end of the bridleway, emerge on a lane and turn right. Pause to admire the view of Ewelme and then

Ewelme watercress beds have now become a local nature reserve. This runs the whole length of the village and contains many wild flowers.

Continue along the High Street, passing an interesting variety of architecture, eventually passing the lane you came down earlier and then the splendid Ewelme Church of England primary school on your left.

The school and almshouses were built in 1437 by William de la Pole and his wife Alice, who was the granddaughter of Geoffrey Chaucer. The school is sometimes open to the public. Telephone 01491 839240 for dates.

7 Continue to reach the cricket pitch and car park on your right.

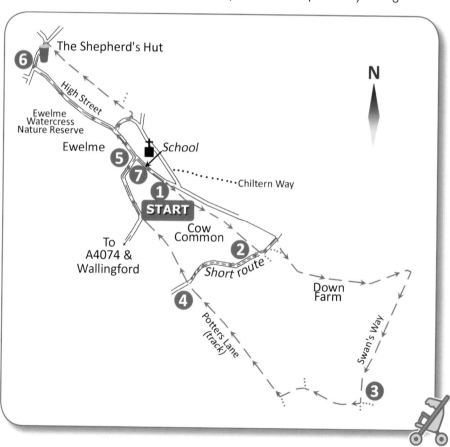

Russell's Water and Maidensgrove Common

See the kites flying

Striding out over the common.

This walk offers amazing views over the Chilterns. Russell's Water and Maidensgrove Common is an enormous area of open grassland, great for seeing wildlife, particularly red kites. If you fancy the other type of kite, you can hire them from the pub at Maidensgrove. There are good blackberry and sloe-picking opportunities in the autumn. You can also feed the ducks at Russell's Water. This is not a long walk and is therefore suitable for all the family; older children can ride bikes or scooters on the common.

Distance: 1½ miles.

Time: Allow 45 minutes.

Terrain: Good grassy paths, tracks and a lane. The paths are good in all but the most inclement weather; however, the whole route is very exposed to the elements, so dress warmly on cold days.

Start/Parking: Take the A4130 from Henley towards Nettlebed and then turn right on the B480 towards Stonor. At Stonor turn left to Maidensgrove, following the road uphill through the woods to reach the common at the top of the hill. Park on the side of the common, near the track signposted to Nuttall's Farm, opposite the entrance to Cookley Hill Farm, RG9 6EX. **OS map:** Explorer 171 Chiltern Hills West; GR SU712889.

Refreshments: The Five Horseshoes pub at Maidensgrove has wonderful views from its garden and high chairs are available, as well as baby-changing facilities. ✆ 01491 641282.

Suggested picnic spot: Anywhere on the common or by the duck pond at Russell's Water.

The Walk

❶ Take the gravel track signposted to Nuttall's Farm. After about 75 metres, turn left along a grassy path, heading for a gap between trees and bushes. The path bears right and then dips down and back up again. Go under a telegraph wire and then after another 100 metres (with a farm over to your right but before you reach a circular bushy area), turn left to skirt round the bushes, to find a footpath through a gap in the bushes, which heads between fences and then between hedges.

Russell's Water and Maidensgrove Common is 400 acres of land where you can walk, cycle, ride or take part in any activity that does not require an engine.

2 At a cross-path, follow the path around to the right, soon emerging on a gravel drive, which leads to Russell's Water village green. Fork right here and then turn right along

The delightful duck pond at Russell's Water.

the road to reach a duck pond.

The duck pond appeared in the film of Chitty Chitty Bang Bang *with Dick van Dyke.*

3 Continue along the road to the far side of the pond and bear right along a gravel drive, just before the village sign. Immediately after passing Pond Cottage on your left, turn left along a bridleway, passing several more houses, and then go ahead between hedgerows to reach the common.

4 Turn right and follow the grassy path along the edge of the bushes, soon crossing a gravel track, and continue along the grassy path ahead. You are soon retracing your footsteps from earlier in the walk but somehow the common takes on a whole new loveliness in a different direction.

You would be unlucky not to see any red kites on this walk. They were reintroduced to the Chilterns in the 1990s, having completely died out in England in the 19th century, when they were considered vermin and churchwardens used to give a penny for every red kite killed.

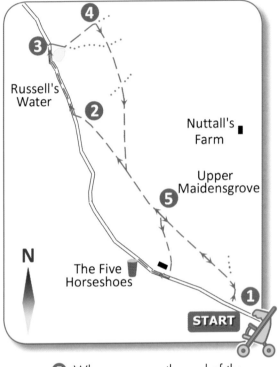

5 When you pass the end of the bushes and can see the hedge that runs next to the road, you may wish to make a short detour to the pub (see below). Otherwise, continue along the grassy path until you reach the gravel track, at which you turn right to return to your car.

To visit the pub: At end of bushes, bear right along a grassy track, heading to the left of a house. Turn right along the lane to reach the Five Horseshoes on your left. The views from the pub garden are simply stunning.

Spade Oak Lake and Little Marlow

A Thames-side and lakeside stroll

St John the Baptist church, Little Marlow.

A **lovely riverside walk,** plus some woodland, a meander round the pretty village of Little Marlow, perhaps a stop for lunch, followed by an amble round Spade Oak Lake.

③

Distance: 2¼ miles.
Time: 1 hour.
Terrain: Mainly footpaths. Suitable for summer only.
Start/Parking: The free public car park in Coldmoorholme Lane, Bourne End, SL8 5PS. From the A404, heading towards Bourne End on the A4155, turn right down Coldmoorholme Lane (signpost for 'Old Thatch'). Go past Old Thatch Gardens and the Spade Oak pub to reach the car park on the right-hand side. **OS map:** Explorer 172 Chiltern Hills East; GR SU884876.
Refreshments: The Spade Oak pub has a large outdoor seating area and highchairs are available. ✆ 01628 520090. The Old Thatch Gardens are open on certain days during the summer. There is a café but no other facilities. ✆ 01628 527518. The Queen's Head at the end of point 3 has a garden and highchairs are available. ✆ 01628 482927.
Suggested picnic spot: Along the river.

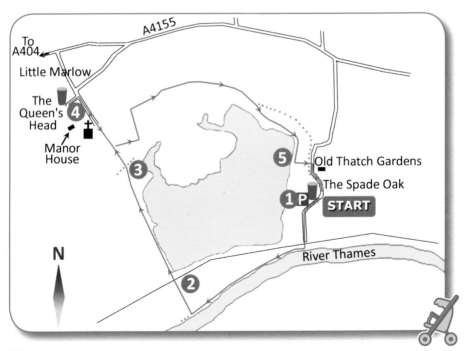

Horses grazing on Spade Oak Nature Reserve.

The Walk

1 From the car park, turn right along the road to go through a metal gate. Cross the railway line and then turn right along the river. Go through a large kissing-gate into a field and continue along the river to walk the length of the field. At the end of the field, go through another kissing-gate and immediately turn right, walking along a hedge.

Spade Oak Wharf was where goods

arrived from London in medieval times. At the end of the 19th century, it had become a popular destination for Londoners taking the Great Western Railway to Marlow or Bourne End. There used to be a ferry across the river here too.

2 Go through a kissing-gate, back across the railway line, through a metal gate and straight on down a track through some trees, with a lake over to your right. Continue in this direction, eventually passing a house with a yellow door, and then continue along a lane.

3 Cross a track giving access to sewage treatment works and go over two ramps. Then look out for a public footpath on your right, which you do not take now but will return to later. Head straight on over a stream and into Little Marlow. Even if you do not have plans to visit the pub, it is worth taking a little look at this delightful village. Pass a flint wall surrounding Little Marlow Manor and then turn left down Pound Lane to reach the Queen's Head pub.

Little Marlow was once home to a 13th-century convent of Benedictine nuns, which belonged to nearby Bisham Abbey. After the dissolution under Henry VIII, the buildings fell derelict and were destroyed by the 18th century, although there are some remains in the village.

4 When you are ready, return through the village to the footpath you spotted earlier and turn left here. Go across a wooden footbridge and along a gravelly path, with a stream on your left. Cross a second footbridge and turn right, with a field on your left. At the end of the field, cross a road ('Lafarge' sign) and go through a metal gate opposite. Walk along the right-hand side of the

field and then straight ahead along a footpath, with a fence on your left and a wood on your right. When you reach a waymark post, turn right into the woods, across a footbridge and, after 10 metres, turn left at a waymark post. The path weaves round to reach a lake, which you keep on your right.

This is Spade Oak Nature Reserve, which was opened in 2002. This former gravel pit is now home to a variety of water birds, including grey heron and red warblers. You should also see some beautiful wild flowers.

5 Pass a sign for Spade Oak Nature Reserve and then turn left across a wooden bridge to go through a gate and across a field. At the end of the field, go through a kissing-gate, which is on the small side but manageable with a bit of wiggling. Emerge on a lane, opposite the entrance to Old Thatch Gardens. Turn right to pass the Spade Oak pub and return to the car park on the right-hand side.

Old Thatch is the former home of Enid Blyton, who described it as a 'fairy tale house'. You can visit the gardens, which have been lovingly restored by the current owners and which feature Blyton's old rose arbour, as well as a number of more contemporary settings.

Hambleden Lock and Aston

Stunning views in the Hambleden valley

The Thames at Hambleden.

This is much more than a pleasant riverside walk, as the views of the Hambleden valley are simply stunning. Children will love the power of the water at Hambleden Weir and you will be spoilt for choice of suitable picnic sites. This walk really is almost entirely on paved paths, with a short grassy section along the Thames just after the lock, which I have always managed even in bad weather so this is an all-year-round walk.

Distance: 3½ miles.

Time: Allow 1½ hours.

Terrain: Mostly paved paths. Approximately 600 metres of grass along the Thames Path, muddy but still passable in winter.

Start/Parking: If approaching on the A4155, start at Mill End free car park, Skirmett Road, south of Hambleden, where there are toilets, with baby-changing facilities. **OS map:** Explorer 171 Chiltern Hills West; GR SU785854. Or, if approaching on the A4130, you could start at the Flower Pot pub, Ferry Lane, Aston, RG9 3DG (GR SU785842) – see point 5. Please check with the landlord before leaving your car in the pub car park.

Refreshments: The Flower Pot, Aston, has a large garden that is great for children and often has barbecues on summer weekends. Buggies are not allowed inside the pub. ∅ 01491 574721. There is usually an ice-cream van by Hambleden Lock on summer weekends.

Suggested picnic spot: Anywhere along the Thames.

Crossing the weir.

The Walk

The description begins from Mill End car park. If you are starting at the Flower Pot in Aston, turn right (past the overflow car park) and go through a large kissing-gate and then continue from point 5 below.

1 Turn right along the pavement to reach and cross the A4155. Follow the footpath sign to Hambleden Weir. Cross the weir and lock, and then turn right.

Hambleden Mill is mentioned in the Domesday Book, which suggests that there may have been a weir then too. The lock was built in 1773 and the lock-keeper's house in 1777. The first lock-keeper, Caleb Gould, was an eccentric man who ate onion porridge every night. Sadly, I do not have the recipe!

2 Soon go through a bridlegate on your left and turn right again, keeping the river on your right, to walk along the Thames Path. This grassy path soon turns to asphalt. Keep walking along the path, passing Greenlands, a white country house on the opposite bank of the river, and then pass Temple Island.

The Temple on Temple Island is a folly, originally designed by James Wyatt as a fishing lodge for Fawley Court, and built in 1771. It marks the start of the course for the Henley Royal Regatta.

3 Opposite Temple Island, you will cross a small cattle grid (it is suitable for wheels). Continue along the Thames until you reach some buildings and trees on your left. Look out for a footpath sign, at which you turn left through a bridlegate and then go through a large kissing-gate and along a track into Remenham.

4 You soon pass a large metal gate and emerge onto a lane. Go straight ahead, passing St Nicholas' church on your left, and then turn left at a T-junction to skirt round the church. At the next junction, stay on this lane, ignoring the road going uphill to the right. Continue along this quiet lane to reach Aston village and then the Flower Pot pub on the left-hand side.

5 Turn left at a footpath sign

just before the Flower Pot and go through a large kissing-gate and along a paved path across fields towards the river.

Children may get a chance to see hens and pigs in the small enclosure behind the pub.

6 When you reach the river, continue along the path to Hambleden Lock. Cross the lock and then the bridges over the weir. **If you started at Aston**, you can turn

around here (unless you need the toilet or baby-changing facilities, which are at Mill End car park), crossing back over the weir and lock and turning right along the Thames Path – see point 2.

7 **To continue to Mill End**, go along the footpath past the boat shed to reach the road. Cross the road with care and take the lane opposite. Walk along the pavement for about 300 metres to reach Mill End car park.

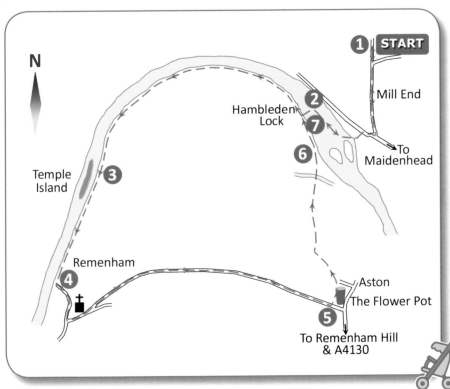

Cookham

In the footsteps of Ratty and Mole

Thatched Cromwell Cottage in Cookham Dean.

Home of Kenneth Grahame and therefore also the birthplace of all the *Wind in the Willows* characters, Cookham is a wonderful place to explore with small children. On this walk, you will head out to the well-heeled Cookham Dean, uphill past allotments to get some fabulous views, through a golf course and then either across the moor or down a bridleway back to the village shops.

Buggy Friendly Walks in The Thames Valley

Distance: 3¾ miles; short option: 2¾ miles.
Time: 1¾ hours; short option: 1¼ hours.
Terrain: Lanes and footpaths. The long route goes across Cookham Moor and is suitable for summer only. The short route avoids the moor but does go across the golf course, so should be fine whenever the weather is suitable for golf.
Start/Parking: The free public car park next to Cookham station, by the shops, SL6 9BT. Alternative parking is available at Cookham Moor on the long route (see end of point 5). Head along the A4094 towards Cookham. When you reach Cookham village, turn off westwards along the High Street and through the village, then past Cookham Moor and into Cookham Rise, where you will find the car park on the left just before the station. **OS map:** Explorer 172 Chiltern Hills East; GR SU887850.
Refreshments: Station Hill Café at the start of the walk has highchairs and baby-changing facilities. ✆ 01628 522202. As well as the café, Cookham has numerous pubs, including the White Oak and the Old Swan Uppers towards the end of the walk.
Suggested picnic spot: Cookham Moor.

The Walk

❶ From the station, turn left along the road, go over the level crossing and continue past the post office, medical centre and Catholic church. Cross over Bradcutts Lane on your right and continue in this direction with fields on your right, eventually reaching the larger, more interesting houses of Cookham Dean.

Kenneth Grahame, beloved author of The Wind in the Willows, *spent his childhood at The Mount (now Herries School) in Cookham Dean,* *so it seems a fair assumption that the characters and settings in the book were inspired by local people and places. Toad of Toad Hall is said to have been based on Colonel Ricardo, who drove a yellow Rolls Royce, the first car in the village.*

❷ At a small junction with a couple of half-timbered cottages and a bench, turn sharp right along Alleyns Lane. Head uphill, soon passing allotments on your left. At the top, turn left along Bradcutts Lane. At a give-way sign, bear right and then right again along Terrys Lane. Look

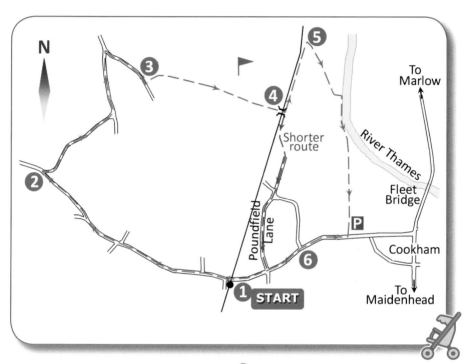

out for a footpath on your left, just before September Grange.

❸ Turn left along this path, immediately going through a gap in the barbed wire fence to walk along the easy grassy path to the left of the fence. At a waymark post, go through a gap in the wooden fence, following the Chiltern Way across the golf course. In good weather, you will have fabulous views here. Head gently downhill, following red footpath signs across the golf course. Eventually cross a bridge over the railway line.

❹ **For the short route:** turn right after the bridge, on the grassy path that takes you along the edge of the golf course, with views of Cookham Moor to your left. Eventually go through a gap in the fence and continue across a small car park to reach a lane where you turn left and then immediately turn right onto a gravel drive (Poundfield Lane). This takes you past some large houses and then downhill, passing a metal gate. Continue along a gravel footpath, which leads to a road where you turn right and skip to point 6.

For the longer route: turn left after the bridge, along a gravelly path downhill, which soon flattens out into an easier grassy path. When you are near the corner of the golf course, skirt round the tee to reach a gravel path ahead (thereby avoiding steps at the end of the footpath). Turn left along the gravel path, go through a wooden gate and immediately turn right through a wooden kissing-gate (lift the metal bar to fold back the gate for your buggy to fit through).

5 Cross a brook and a concrete square and bear right along a path roughly following the line of telegraph poles. This well-worn grassy path eventually leads to the Moor car park. Go through the car park and cross the road. Head up the slope to turn right over the bridge and continue in this direction (heading towards the station).

The bridge you have just walked over is the Fleet Bridge, which was built in 1929 and was the subject of a Stanley Spencer painting in 1937. Stanley Spencer painted lots of Cookham scenes, many of which can be seen in the Stanley Spencer Gallery in Cookham High Street.

6 When you reach the White Oak pub, cross at the zebra crossing and continue along the right-hand pavement, which is narrow in places but just wide enough for a buggy. Pass the Old Swan Uppers pub and then Poundfield Lane (**short route** rejoins here). Continue in this direction to

Cookham village.

return to the station and your car.

Swan Upping is a medieval
ceremony that takes place during the
third week of July.

The Queen's Swan Marker and
his team of Uppers head along the
Thames from Sunbury to Abingdon,
marking all the cygnets and taking a
census of the swan population.

6

Burnham Beeches

A walk through ancient woodland

The woodland floor.

This is a wonderful walk through ancient woodland, with excellent paths for pushchairs and plenty of playing and exploring opportunities for older children. There are some gentle hills and you should expect a little bit of mud if there has been rain recently. Although the paths are good, they can be bumpy in places so do make sure your little ones are strapped in!

Distance: 2¾ miles (if you take the shortcut, it is only 1¾ miles).
Time: Allow 1¼ hours for the full route.
Terrain: Woodland tracks and tarmac paths. This walk can be muddy in winter. However, you can walk the tarmac path all year round; it is easy to follow and does not require a map (although you can get one from the information centre).
Start/Parking: The free car park by Beeches Café and Information Point on Lord Mayor's Drive, off Beeches Road, just off the A355 in Farnham Common. Well signposted from Farnham Common or Burnham.
OS map: Explorer 172 Chiltern Hills East; GR SU956851.
Refreshments: Beeches Café, an outdoor café, at the start of the walk, where there is plenty of room for pushchairs. A toilet block, with baby-changing facilities, is available next to the information centre.
Suggested picnic spot: The large grassy area by the car park (also suitable for ball games etc); the clearing by Druid's Oak at point 2.

The Walk

❶ From the café, turn left along Lord Mayor's Drive towards a large metal gate by the Victory Cross board. Go through the gate and immediately bear left along a track, which soon has a wire fence along the left-hand side.

❷ At cross-tracks, turn left downhill to reach Upper Pond. Continue with the pond on your left, straight on at the next cross-tracks (there is now a small stream on your left). You will soon see Middle Pond on your left. At the end of Middle Pond, bear right. At a Y-junction, bear right towards a clearing in which you will find the Druid's Oak, an

800-year-old pollard, the oldest tree in Burnham Beeches.

Pollarding is a medieval method of pruning trees that produces wood for poles or fodder to feed livestock. Trees are pruned at intervals of several years and this keeps them in a juvenile state, which encourages them to live longer and explains why some of these pollards in Burnham Beeches are so old. In Victorian times, many of the pollards were given names, such as the Druids Oak.

❸ Walk across the clearing to reach a tarmac path, at which you turn left. Go through a metal gate, then immediately turn right in front of a wooden shelter.

This was a checkpoint during the Second World War when the woods were requisitioned by the army and used as a Vehicle Reserve Depot. Hundreds of vehicles used in the D-Day landings passed through Burnham Beeches.

4 Ignore the gate ahead but stay on the track, keeping the wooden fence on your right, until you reach a small triangle. Turn left here and walk downhill. At the bottom of the hill you will reach cross-tracks where you turn right. Keep going until you

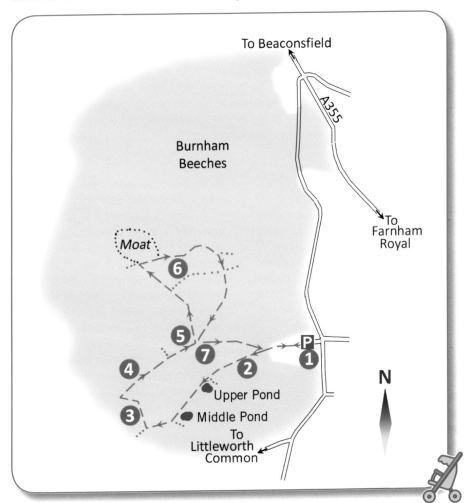

Approaching one of the many pollarded oaks.

reach a junction with a tarmac path and a little wooden hut. **Shortcut:** you can take a shortcut here by turning right and skipping to point 7.

5 Turn left along the tarmac path, which goes gently uphill (though this can be hard work with a buggy – luckily, there are two benches on the way up!). At the top of the hill, continue along the tarmac drive, ignoring the first tarmac path to your right and Woods Drive to your left, until you reach a second tarmac path on your right, McAuliffe Drive (opposite a small wooden hut). Turn right along McAuliffe Drive.

Hartley Court Moat on your left dates from the 12th/14th centuries. It contained a farmstead or homestead and was designed to protect the homestead from deer and swine.

6 Continue along this tarmac path, which eventually curves round to the right and then goes gently downhill to a junction with Dukes Drive and a large wooden sign (Burnham Walk). Go straight across to the track opposite going downhill. This track crosses a stream at the bottom of the hill and then rises gently to reach a track junction of five paths. Take the path straight ahead and eventually reach a small wooden hut and tarmac drive (you were here before at the start of point 5), where you turn left uphill.

7 Walk up the tarmac drive and eventually return to Victory Cross, where you bear left to reach the café and your car.

7

Highmoor

An ancient beech wood and the Nettlebed Estate

Looking towards Highmoor Common Wood.

This walk offers a wonderful mixture of English woodlands and open views. The ancient woodland of Highmoor Common Wood includes beech, cherry and hornbeam, and there is a carpet of bluebells here in season. The route continues through the Nettlebed Estate, owned by the Fleming family. Ian Fleming is thought to have written one of the first James Bond books nearby and his aunt Celia Johnson (of *Brief Encounter* fame) is buried in Nettlebed churchyard. The surrounding woodland here puts on a stunning display of rhododendrons in May/June.

Distance: 3¼ miles.
Time: Allow 1¼ hours.
Terrain: A mixture of paved paths and bridleways, which can get muddy in winter.
Start/Parking: The Dog and Duck pub, Highmoor, RG9 5DL. Take the A4130, which runs between Wallingford and Henley and turn off southwards on the B481. Shortly after entering Highmoor village, you will see the pub on your left. Please check with the landlord before leaving your car in the pub car park. OS map: Explorer 171 Chiltern Hills West; GR SU701848.
Refreshments: The Dog and Duck pub has a lovely garden, with a children's play area that includes a baby swing. Highchairs are also available. ✆ 01491 641261.
Suggested picnic spot: You could have a teddy bears' picnic in the woods.

The Walk

❶ From the Dog and Duck car park, facing the main road, turn right along the restricted byway, which leads into the woods. Pass Tudor Cottage on your right and continue straight on, ignoring a fork to your right, until you reach a 5-way junction with a signpost.

❷ Go straight ahead in the direction of Merrimoles House. Ignore a fork to your right and continue straight ahead. When you reach a track junction at a pylon, turn right along the restricted byway, soon passing a large house on your right. Continue along an enclosed track, which has fields on

either side and then bears left as you enter more woodland. The track descends to a T-junction, where you turn right.

❸ You now have a field on your left and a wood on your right. Continue along this track for ½ mile until you reach a junction with a waymark post with purple arrows on it. Here you turn right, uphill into woodland. The track soon curves left and becomes a tarmac path. Pass houses on your right and then emerge onto open land with lovely views of the surrounding woodland. Continue on this tarmac path for another 500 metres to reach a crossroads (sign for Bromsden Farm straight ahead) at which you turn right.

4 Walk along this bridleway to pass through a gate next to a cattle grid and then continue along this path, which now curves to the left, passing a copse in an old pit on your left. Continue along this metalled path for ½ mile to reach another cattle grid.

5 Go through a gate to the left of the cattle grid and then immediately turn right along a track into the woods. The track soon passes a metal gate and then continues between rhododendron and holly bushes, with

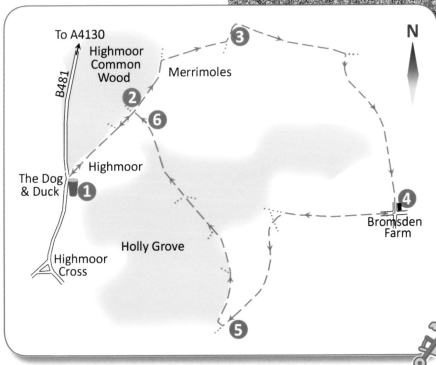

The woods are a mass of bluebells in late spring.

the edge of the wood on your right. Keep straight on and you will soon be surrounded by thick woodland; here rhododendrons flower in season. Stay on this stony track, ignoring all paths to the left and right. The path eventually leaves the wood and continues between hedges.

❻ Pass a white house on your left and soon reach the 5-way junction (which you encountered near the start of the walk). Take the second left (10 o'clock), now retracing your steps along the metalled path back to the pub.

Checkendon and Stoke Row

A walk fit for a Maharajah

The Maharajah's Well at Stoke Row.

This is a fairly adventurous walk, due to the distance, variety of terrain and the odd undulation. There is a lot to see, including the famous Maharajah's Well and cherry orchard (beautiful blossom in spring), pretty cottages, woods, and animals grazing. You have a choice of lovely country pubs, as well as a delightful picnic spot in the orchard next to the Maharajah's Well where you are allowed to pick cherries in season.

Distance: 4½ miles.
Time: Allow 2 hours, plus stopping time.
Terrain: A mixture of footpaths, lanes and woodland tracks. The paths can get muddy and churned by horses so this is a walk recommended for summer only.
Start/Parking: Park by the church of St Peter and St Paul in Checkendon, RG8 0SR. Take the A4074 between Reading and Wallingford. A mile north of Chazey Heath, turn off north-eastwards along Park Lane and continue for approximately 2 miles to reach Checkendon. OS map: Explorer 171 Chiltern Hills West; GR SU664830.
Refreshments: The Four Horseshoes pub at Checkendon is run by the lovely people who own the Dog and Duck in Highmoor. It has highchairs, a large garden and a children's playground. ✆ 01491 680325. The Cherry Tree Inn in Stoke Row has a garden, high chairs and baby-changing facilities. ✆ 01491 680325. There is also a village shop in Stoke Row.
Suggested picnic spot: By the Maharajah's Well; in the cherry orchard next to it; or by the playground in Checkendon.

The Walk

❶ From the church, turn left along the pavement, past the primary school. Cross the road to the pavement opposite and continue in the same direction, walking alongside the playing fields. Note that there is a playground with picnic tables and baby swings further along. Pass a red telephone box and cross Whitehall Lane on your right.

Checkendon is a very pretty Oxfordshire village, with some lovely timber-framed buildings near the church. Look out for the old post office across the road from the church and the old smithy, which is now a car repair business.

❷ When the pavement ends, turn left along a lane towards Ipsden and the Equestrian Centre. This is a 'quiet lane'. Pass a farmhouse and the Equestrian Centre and continue along the lane. At a junction 200 metres later, turn right along a lane towards Ipsden and Nuffield. Pass a farm on your right and then immediately turn right along a track (do not take the footpath across the grass). You are walking along the edge of some woodland. After 200

41

metres, at a waymark post, continue towards a cottage and then just before the cottage, turn left along a track into the woods. The main track, which is often churned by horses, joins from your left. Bear right along this and soon reach a house and gravel track. Bear right along this track, which leads to a lane where you turn right.

The 12th-century church of St Peter and St Paul, Checkendon.

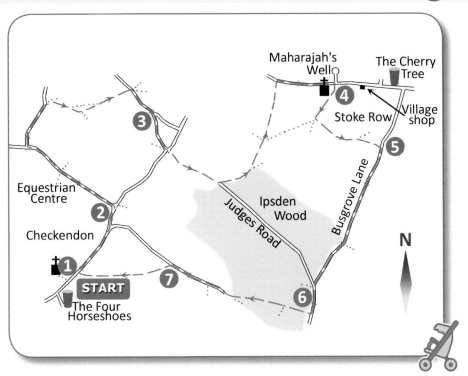

3 At a fork in the lane, bear right and then at a road, cross to a bridleway opposite (gravel track). Pass a house on your right and 20 metres later reach a path junction. Turn left here. The path goes uphill and at the top you fork left. Soon you have a fence on your right and can glimpse fields through the trees to your left. When the fence ends, the path bears slightly right and is soon joined by another fence on your right. At a gap in the fence, turn left, away from the fence and 20 metres later, turn right along an obvious path through the woods. This soon

becomes a gravel track. Go past a metal barrier and straight ahead to reach a road and turn right along the pavement, crossing to the other side when the pavement switches sides. You are now in Stoke Row. Continue past the church and school to reach the Maharajah's Well on the left-hand side.

The Maharajah's Well was built in 1863–4. It is a massive 368 ft (112 metres) deep and was dug entirely by hand. The benefactor was an Indian nobleman, the Maharajah of Benares, who had heard about the water shortages in the area and wanted to provide the villagers with 'the privilege of taking water free of charge, in all time to come'. He also bought the land for the neighbouring cherry orchard, so that the profits from selling cherries could be used to fund the upkeep of the well.

Stoke Row amenities: The village shop is a little further along on the right-hand side. The Cherry Tree pub is ¼ mile further on the left, just after passing Busgrove Lane on your right. If you visit the shop or pub, do not retrace your steps to the well but instead head down Busgrove Lane and skip to point 5.

Stoke Row was only a little hamlet prior to the well being built but grew during the later Victorian years. Local industry included brickmaking and also the production of tent pegs, which continued until the Second World War.

4 From the well, turn right back along the main road and then turn left along School Lane, just before the church. Immediately after Number 12 on the left-hand side, turn left down a footpath, which eventually leads into woods, mainly holly bushes. Continue in this direction and eventually reach a lane.

5 Turn right along the lane (Busgrove Lane), passing a 'quiet lane' sign, which you will follow for just over ½ mile. The lane goes downhill then passes a track on your left, a track on your right and then a muddy bridleway on your right. Continue along the lane as it bends to the right and reaches a junction, where you turn right along a lane, passing another 'quiet lane' sign.

6 Continue slightly uphill along this lane, eventually emerging from the woods and passing Lilac House on your right. Look out for Shire horses in the field on your right. Once you reach the houses, soon after passing Orchard Lodge on your right, look out for a metal kissing-gate in the hedge on your left.

7 Go through the gate and head across the field on a grassy path to a kissing-gate in the opposite corner. Go through the kissing-gate and straight ahead along a path to the right of a metal gate. Go through the woods, staying left at a fork and continue in the same general direction, eventually reaching a track junction with a hut on your right. Turn right to skirt round the hut and walk along the left-hand side of the cricket field to reach a road and turn left to return to the church and your car. The Four Horseshoes pub is 200 metres farther along the lane.

Dew Drop Inn and Hall Place

Enjoy those fabulous views

The pub that is said to have been a haunt of the highwayman, Dick Turpin.

This walk takes you into the grounds of Hall Place, across fields and into High Wood, where you get some amazing views over the Thames Valley. Then it is back to Honey Lane and up a bridleway to the Dew Drop Inn for some refreshment.

Distance: 2¾ miles.

Time: 1¼ hours.

Terrain: Footpaths and tracks. These can get muddy, so a walk best kept for summer only.

Start/Parking: Dew Drop Inn, Honey Lane, Hurley, SL6 6RB. From the A404, turn off at signs for the A4130 towards Henley. At the first roundabout, follow the signs for Burchett's Green. Go through Burchett's Green and turn right onto Honey Lane (signposted 'Dew Drop Inn'). Follow this lane for 1 mile until it bends sharply to the right and you go straight on to reach the Dew Drop Inn on your right. Please check with the landlord before leaving your car in the pub car park.

OS map: Explorer 172 Chiltern Hills East; GR SU823815.

Refreshments: The Dew Drop Inn has a garden and highchairs are available. ✆ 01628 824327.

Suggested picnic spot: Overlooking the valley at High Wood.

The Walk

1 From the Dew Drop Inn, turn left out of the car park, left along the lane across the top of the pub garden and then left down Honey Lane. Pass some houses on your left and then take a tarmac drive on your right, which is also a permissive path into the grounds of Hall Place.

2 Walk along the tarmac path, past Calves Leys Wood on your right. Then look out for a footpath crossing your path and turn left here. Walk along this grassy path and cross over a gravel track to head along a second field towards the trees. At the end of the second field, you reach High Wood and go

through a metal kissing-gate into the wood.

High Wood is an ancient woodland including beech, ash and hazel. This type of woodland would have covered the Thames Valley in the Middle Ages, when the River Thames was the main transport link.

3 Continue in the same direction along a woodland track to reach the end of the wood and turn right just before a kissing-gate, keeping a fence on your left, with lovely views over the valley to your left. When the footpath bends to the right, so

do you. Follow this path through the wood and through a kissing-gate to a field. Go straight ahead and down the grass track until you reach a track junction, where you turn right along a gravel path.

Hall Place is home to the Berkshire College of Agriculture, which owns all the grounds you are walking in. The original building was constructed in the 13th century as the manor house of Hurley but this was destroyed by William East in the 18th century and he built a Georgian mansion in its place. You can continue along the footpath

The glorious countryside surrounding Hurley.

47

ahead to take a look at the manor house but you will have to return the way you came as that is the only public right of way.

4 At the next track junction, turn left, back along the grassy footpath you walked earlier and turn right at the tarmac drive to return to Honey Lane.

5 Go straight across the lane to a bridleway, which you follow, first left and then right, until you reach a track junction. Turn left here, ignoring footpaths on either side, to return to the Dew Drop Inn.

The Dew Drop Inn was once a regular haunt of Dick Turpin, who apparently used to hide his horse Black Bess in the cellars when he stayed here.

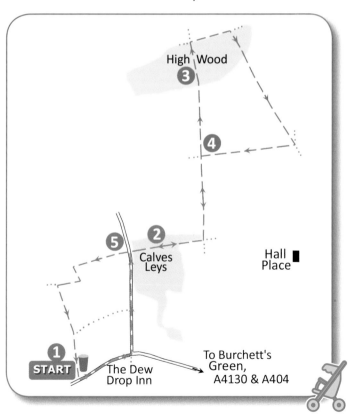

Maidenhead Thicket and Littlewick Green

Two pretty villages and an ancient wood

Littlewick Green.

This lovely circuit is a proper country walk that just happens to have no obstacles to buggies. You start in the Thicket, which comes as a surprise to those who haven't encountered it before, so close to Maidenhead. Then it's across some fields to Burchett's Green and along a bridleway to reach Littlewick Green, a charming village where cricket is often being played at weekends in summer. A good cycle path and lane bring you back towards the Thicket, with an optional stop at the Shire Horse, a very family-friendly pub, just ½ mile from the end of the walk.

Distance: 4 miles.
Time: Allow 1½ hours.
Terrain: Footpaths, tracks, lanes and cycle path. Maidenhead Thicket can be muddy so be careful if considering this walk after a period of heavy rain (an alternative route, avoiding the Thicket section at the end of the walk, is described below).
Start/Parking: The free public car park on Stubbings Road, Maidenhead. From the A404, take the A4 into Maidenhead and at the first roundabout turn left towards Stubbings and after 200 metres turn left into the car park. **OS map:** Explorer 172 Chiltern Hills East; GR SU858810.
Refreshments: The Shire Horse, in point 5 of the walk, has highchairs, baby-changing facilities and a large garden. ✆ 01628 876189. The Crown, Burchett's Green, (✆ 01628 826184) is close to point 3 of the walk and the Cricketers, Littlewick Green (✆ 01628 822888) is passed in point 4.
Suggested picnic spot: On the village green at Littlewick Green.

The Walk

❶ From the car park, take the footbridge over the busy A404 and into the Thicket. On entering the Thicket, turn right along a (sometimes muddy) path that runs along the edge of the Thicket and soon widens. After about 100 metres you will reach a track; this was once a metalled path and is still quite easy for a buggy, though now somewhat overgrown. Turn left along this track, heading towards a red-brick lodge at the end.

Maidenhead Thicket was once notorious for highwaymen, who were often in cahoots with the landlords of the local hostelries, who passed on details of travellers who could soon be divested of their property.

❷ Pass to the right of the lodge and cross a little lane to a buggy-friendly kissing-gate opposite. Through the kissing-gate, continue straight ahead between two lines of trees to reach another kissing-gate. Go through the second kissing-gate to reach an open field and continue straight ahead along the path, first with a fence on your left and then between fields. At the end of the field, go through a farmyard to reach a lane. This is Burchett's Green. If you would like to stop here, turn right along the lane to reach the Crown pub.

❸ Otherwise, turn left along the lane and walk out of the village, passing the 'no limit' sign. Turn right at the sign for Knowl Hill Bridle Circuit. This bridleway soon becomes a lane. Continue along this lane until you reach the busy A4.

❹ Cross the A4 with care and take the lane opposite into Littlewick Green. Upon reaching the green, you can choose to walk either straight across or around it (take the right-hand path to reach the Cricketers pub) but finish on the far left-hand side, outside Ivor Novello's house.

Ivor Novello was a Welsh singer, songwriter and actor, who wrote the famous Keep the Home Fires Burning *at the start of the First World War. He purchased Redroofs in Littlewick Green in the 1920s and held notoriously unconventional parties here, entertaining Noel Coward and other celebrities of the time.*

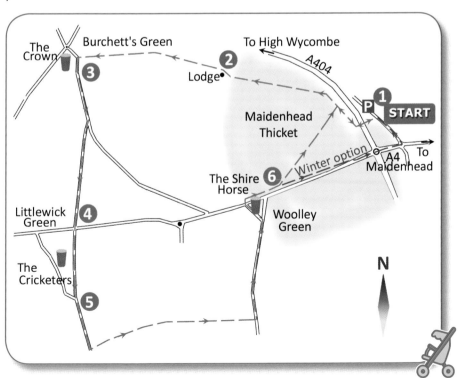

5 Continue along School Lane, past the Montessori School. The lane turns into a track, which goes through some trees and emerges onto another lane, where you turn left. Continue in this direction as the lane becomes a cycle path. Cross over a minor road, and continue along the cycle path, heading towards a large pale house. At the end of the cycle path, you reach a lane and turn left. Pass some pretty houses and continue along the lane until you can hear the traffic of the A4 ahead. The path forks. Take the left fork to reach the Shire Horse pub. From the pub, cross the main road carefully and turn right along the pavement. After 50 metres, turn left at a public footpath sign (opposite Cherry Garden Lane). **NB:** If the thicket is muddy, it is possible to avoid it by continuing along the pavement next to the A4, crossing straight over the roundabout and then left at the next roundabout. You will reach the car park after about 200 metres.

The A4 used to be the Maidenhead turnpike road, where tolls were collected at gates. In the 1860s, the gates were removed and an avenue of lime trees was planted along the Bath Road, many of which are still standing.

6 To continue the walk through the Thicket from the footpath sign on the A4, bear slightly right to go down a small slope and reach a track crossing your path. Cross over the track and go straight ahead into the woods. After 30 metres, reach cross-paths with a waymark post. Turn right here and walk along this path with the A4 over to your right.

Pass another waymark post when a path joins from your right. Continue straight ahead. Pass a path on your left and then a small pit on your right. Ignore a right turn immediately after the pit and go left at a fork and then right at a second fork 10 metres later. This path is slightly overgrown in places and is soon joined by a path from your left. Ten metres later, stay left on the main path and eventually emerge onto a wide track crossing your path. Turn right here and then take the first left after 20 metres to return to the footbridge and car park.

Goring

An amble through the Gap

A quiet backwater.

The route starts by heading out into the countryside where you will find a variety of wildlife in the hedgerows. A quick tour of the Thames follows, and then into Goring village with its pretty houses and village shops. There are great sloe and blackberry-picking opportunities in September.

Distance: 2½ miles.

Time: Allow 1 hour.

Terrain: Tarmac paths, stony tracks and then a sometimes muddy path along the Thames, which can be avoided by taking the 'winter' option so this easy-going walk is suitable all year round and in all conditions.

Start/Parking: Goring and Streatley station car park, RG8 0EP (parking charge). Head to Streatley on the A329 from Reading in the south or Wallingford in the north, or the A417 from Wantage. Turn eastwards at traffic lights onto the B4009 to cross the river into Goring; continue to a T-junction where you turn right to reach the station and car park. Note that although you can arrive by train, westbound trains arrive at the middle platform, from which there is no step-free exit from the station.

OS map: Explorer 171 Chiltern Hills West; GR SU603806. Alternative parking is available in the centre of Goring. Follow the parking signs and then start the walk by the public lavatories in point 6.

Refreshments: Pierreponts Café, ½ mile from the end of the walk, has highchairs and baby-changing facilities available. ✆ 01491 874464. The Miller of Mansfield pub, also ½ mile from the end of the walk, has highchairs. ✆ 01491 872829. Toilets are available at the railway station and there are also public toilets in Goring village.

Suggested picnic spot: Along the Thames, just before Goring Lock at point 5.

The Walk

❶ From the car park, facing away from the railway line, turn right up a lane (no through road). Pass the bungalows and continue between fields. Continue along this lane until you see a fork to the right, 'Private drive, bridleway only'; take this path.

❷ Keep to the tarmac path as it bears right (passing a bridleway to Whitchurch on Thames on your left). Soon the footpath turns right in front of a large red-brick house. Pass a metal gate to continue straight on along an overgrown stony path between fields. Go under a railway bridge, through a bridlegate and turn right along a gravelly track, following this track as it bears left and right.

The white house in the trees across the river to your left is The Grotto. The original building was an ornate shell room and rock pool, built in 1720 for the Fane family who owned Basildon Park. Not much remains of the original grotto but Lady Fane is said to have haunted the house since her death.

❸ When the track turns left, go straight ahead between the green posts next to the metal gate and continue on the wide path between the trees.

❹ In 50 metres, you reach a lamppost on your left. **Winter option:**

go straight on along a residential street (Manor Road) right to the end and turn left at the junction and immediately left again (before the florist) along Ferry Lane. Continue to the end of the lane and then ahead between the bollards and then across the grass to reach the river and turn right. **Summer option:** turn left at the lamppost, along a gravel drive. At Waterford Cottage, the footpath forks right between fences and eventually reaches the river. Turn right along the Thames Path for ½ mile. (**Winter option** joins from right,

This walk is suitable in all seasons.

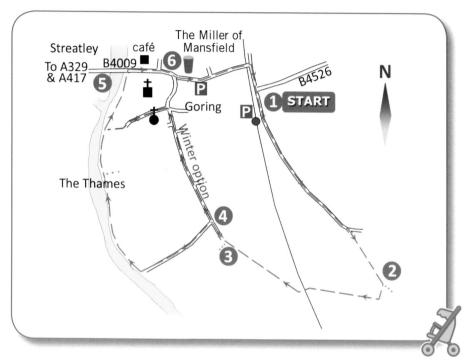

The Miller of Mansfield
Streatley   café
To A329 B4009 ■ 6
& A417 5   ✝
         Goring P
                 P 1 START
B4526
N

Winter option

The Thames

4

3

2

just before a little stone bridge.)

Goring Gap was formed during the last Ice Age when the River Thames changed its course, forming a gorge between the Berkshire Downs and the Chiltern Hills. There is evidence that Goring and Streatley have been continuously inhabited for over 5,000 years. Stone Age man would have travelled here along the Ridgeway and the Icknield Way, two long-distance paths which can still be walked today.

5 When you reach Goring Lock, just before the road bridge goes overhead, turn right along a tarmac path, passing the old water mill, to join the main road. Pierreponts Café is across the road, shortly after the mill.

6 Continue along the main road, passing the Miller of Mansfield pub on your left and then the shops. (A footpath to the public lavatories and to the village centre car park is on the right-hand side after the 'Mary S.' interiors shop.) Go across the railway bridge then turn right to return to the railway station car park.

Lower Shiplake

Harpsden Wood and the Thames Path

Pleasure craft on the Thames.

This fairly strenuous walk starts in Lower Shiplake and takes you along bridleways up to Harpsden Wood, then a short stretch uphill to the outskirts of Henley from where you head to Marsh Lock for a lovely riverside stroll back to the start. Be warned that you may get house envy during some parts of this walk!

Distance: 5 miles.
Time: 2½ hours.
Terrain: Footpaths, lanes and tracks; summer only route.
Start/Parking: Shiplake station car park (free), Station Road, Lower Shiplake, RG9 3NY. Take the A4155 between Henley and Reading; about 2 miles south of Henley, turn off eastwards into Lower Shiplake and follow this road to reach the station at the end. **OS map:** Explorer 171 Chiltern Hills West; GR SU777797.
Refreshments: The Baskerville pub has a lovely garden, barbecues in summer and a climbing frame; highchairs also available. ✆ 0118 940 3332. There is also a village shop opposite the pub.
Suggested picnic spot: Picnic tables by Marsh Lock at the end of point 5 or in Harpsden Wood – see point 3. Note that this stretch of the Thames is not suitable for picnics as there is a lot of undergrowth.

The Walk

❶ From the station car park, cross the level crossing and immediately turn left, following the Thames Path. After about 500 metres, look out for a byway on the left-hand side, just after The White House. Turn left here. The byway takes you back over the railway line and eventually reaches the main road (A4155). Cross the main road to the bridleway opposite.

❷ Head uphill along the bridleway, which starts as a tarmac path and turns into a stony track but then becomes tarmac again, eventually to reach a quiet lane at the top, where you turn right.

You are now in Harpsden Wood,

owned by the Woodland Trust. It is an ancient woodland (which means it is at least 400 years old).

❸ Walk along this lane, passing a 'no limit' sign and then 150 metres later, turn right at a bridleway sign, soon walking with a wire fence on your right. This narrow path soon becomes a lovely woodland track through beeches. The path goes downhill and bears right, where another path joins from your left. At the bottom of the hill, bear left onto a lane before the path gets narrow. Turn right along the lane towards the triangle of grass opposite St Margaret's cemetery and its pretty lychgate. Turn left towards Harpsden (take care along this lane), passing Henley Golf

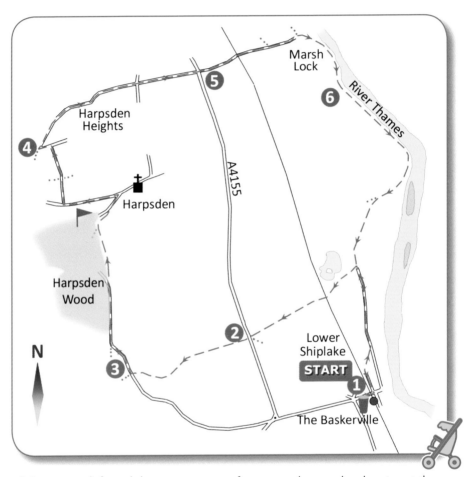

Club on your left and then turn right along a bridleway. Power on uphill to emerge on a lane opposite Greysfield and turn left.

4 At the end of the lane, turn right along a footpath, pushing your buggy under the pi-shaped metal barrier, and walk between the fences, under another barrier at the end and then turn right on Peppard Lane. Keep to this lane, passing streets and cul-de-sacs both left and right. Cross Harpsden Way and continue on the stony track opposite (still Peppard Lane). At the end, take the bridleway straight ahead to reach the main road.

5 Bear slightly right and cross the main road to go down Mill Lane, to the left of the petrol station. Continue over the railway bridge to reach the river. At the river, go straight ahead over the wooden bridge, passing Marsh Lock.

You might notice that the lock is on the opposite side of the river to the towpath, so this wooden bridge had to be built from the Oxfordshire bank to the lock island and back

again to take the towpath past the lock. Although there were several attempts during the 19th century to have the lock moved to the other side of the river, this never materialised.

6 Continue along the Thames Path, following the acorn signs, passing a miniature railway at Thames Side Court, from where the path becomes tarmac and eventually leads back to the level crossing and car park.

The wooden bridge at point 5 of the walk.

Dorney Lake and Two Rivers

A new take on an old favourite

The driveway to Dorney Court.

Dorney Lake, a favourite haunt of new mothers, who doggedly push their prams round the lake in a determined effort to lose the baby weight, is one of the reasons I was inspired to write this book. The lake is very pleasant but three times a week would be too monotonous for me. I couldn't help thinking that there must be something better, and it was probably quite close. The lack of facilities around the lake is a particular drawback, which was brought home to me once when a friend and I were exactly halfway round the lake and our babies both started screaming at the top of their lungs, as babies do. We had no choice but to continue walking, as fast as we could, past the disapproving dog walkers, to return to our car and drive to the nearest pub so that we could feed and change our little ones.

So, here it is, you can have the lake and more! This route takes in a stretch of the Thames Path and a mile alongside the Jubilee River – and there is a lovely café near the end of the walk, plus one in Eton Wick if you can't wait that long.

Distance: 4¾ miles.

Time: Allow 2 hours.

Terrain: Tarmac paths and gravel tracks. Can get slightly muddy in winter but not impassable.

Start/Parking: Park at the free Arboretum's car park, close to the entrance to Dorney Lake, SL4 6QP. From Maidenhead, take the A4 eastbound towards Burnham. After 2 miles, turn right at the roundabout onto the B3026 towards Dorney (following the brown signs to Dorney Lake from now on). As you enter Dorney village, the road bends left and you turn right into Court Lane. Pass Dorney Court on your left and you will see the entrance to Dorney Lake straight ahead. The Arboretum car park is about 100 yards further, on your right. **OS map:** Explorer 160 Windsor, Weybridge & Bracknell; GR SU921788.

Refreshments: Dorney Court Kitchen Garden near the end of the walk has an indoor and outdoor seating area, a climbing frame, highchairs, toilets and baby-changing facilities. ∅ 01628 669999. There is also the Village Bakery and Café in Eton Wick at the end of point 5. ∅ 01753 850499.

Suggested picnic spot: Beside Dorney Lake and along the Jubilee River.

The Walk

1 From the Arboretum car park, head past the information board, across the grass towards the lake. Cross a tarmac drive and continue straight over the grass to reach a tarmac path, which goes round the lake. Turn left and walk alongside the lake towards the Rowing Centre building at the far end.

Dorney Lake, the venue for rowing and kayaking events in the 2012 Olympic Games, is Eton College's rowing centre.

2 Three-quarters of the way along the lake, the trees on the left come closer to the water. Look out for a tarmac road going off to the left which leads to a gate with a sign saying 'Emergency access, keep clear'. Head through this gate and along a gravel drive to a cattle grid. Go through the wooden gate next to the cattle grid and walk straight ahead towards a wooden fence where you turn right along a lane.

3 After 100 metres, turn right towards a car park and go through a large wooden gate, across the car park and ahead over the grass to reach another wooden gate. Go through the gate and turn right to reach Boveney church.

St Mary Magdalene church, Boveney, has an interesting wooden bell tower and walls of rubble and flint. It is currently leased by the Friends of Friendless Churches, who saved it from developers in 1975. Although rarely used, the church is still consecrated and apparently holds three services a year.

The church of St Mary Magdalene, Boveney.

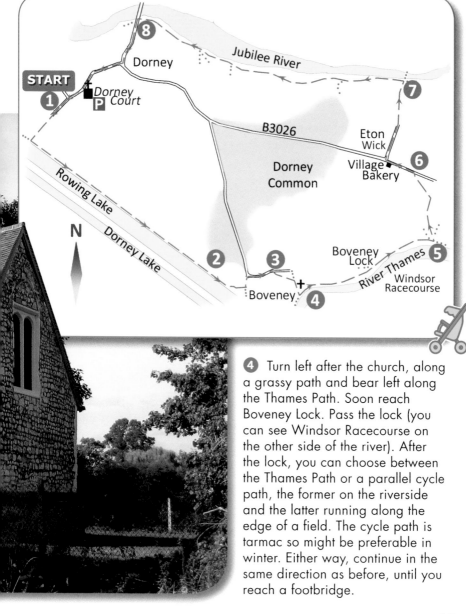

4 Turn left after the church, along a grassy path and bear left along the Thames Path. Soon reach Boveney Lock. Pass the lock (you can see Windsor Racecourse on the other side of the river). After the lock, you can choose between the Thames Path or a parallel cycle path, the former on the riverside and the latter running along the edge of a field. The cycle path is tarmac so might be preferable in winter. Either way, continue in the same direction as before, until you reach a footbridge.

5 Cross the footbridge and turn left along a tarmac path. Soon fork left, keeping a stream on your left, and head towards some playing fields. At the playing fields, bear right along a tarmac path. When you reach some houses, turn left onto a bridleway and continue along the pavement (passing a playground on your left), to pass a modern church and then turn left along the main road.

Eton Wick has a variety of shops, including the Village Bakery and Café, 100 metres ahead on the left-hand side.

6 Unless you are visiting the bakery, cross the main road at the zebra crossing and turn left, continuing along this road until you reach Moores Lane (shortly after passing the bakery), where you turn right. Pass a village green and playground on your left and continue along the pavement until it runs out and go straight ahead between two bollards onto a tarmac bridleway between fields.

7 Just before the bridge, turn left along the cycle path. You are now walking with the Jubilee River on your right for just over a mile. Pass a weir, then ½ mile later, pass a footbridge. Do not head up the bridleway but stick to the

level riverside path. Pass a second footbridge. Keep going until you reach a road. Shortly before the road, go through a metal swing gate and across a car park, through a bridlegate and over the road.

8 Turn left along the pavement and into Dorney village. As the road bends to the left, you turn right along Court Lane. After 50 metres, you will see the entrance to Dorney Court on your left. This leads to Dorney Court Kitchen Garden and Café. After visiting the café (optional, of course!), continue along this lane, past St James the Less church. When the road bends to the right, cross carefully to the entrance to Dorney Lake and walk along the gravel path on the left-hand side of the road. At the information sign, cross the road to return to the Arboretum car park.

Dorney Court is an early Tudor manor house, owned by the Palmer family for the last 450 years. It appeared in the film Lock, Stock and Two Smoking Barrels, *as the country house robbed by the bungling Scousers. A large stone pineapple stands in the Great Hall to commemorate England's first ever pineapple, which is believed to have been grown in Dorney. The garden centre is the old kitchen garden for the house.*

Holyport

A charming village

The sundial at point 3 of the walk.

Starting from Holyport on the outskirts of Maidenhead, this gentle walk is very easy-going and makes an excellent stroll following a pub lunch or perhaps after the Holyport baby and toddler clinic on a Thursday morning. The memorial hall also has a children's playground.

Holyport's charming duck pond.

Distance: 1½ miles.

Time: 40 minutes.

Terrain: Lanes, gravel paths and bridleways, suitable all year round.

Start/Parking: The free car park at Holyport War Memorial Hall, Money Row Green, Holyport SL6 2NA. From Maidenhead, head south along the A330 towards Ascot. Pass the Holyport village sign and turn left at the village green; then turn right along Money Row Green and look for the memorial hall on your right. **OS map:** Explorer 160 Windsor, Weybridge & Bracknell; GR SU892775.

Refreshments: The Belgian Arms pub has a garden that overlooks the duck pond and has highchairs available. ⌀ 01628 634468. The George on the Green also has a garden and highchairs available. ⌀ 01628 628317.

Suggested picnic spot: By the duck pond or at the picnic table in the playground by the memorial hall.

The Walk

1 From Holyport War Memorial Hall, turn left and walk along the pavement until you pass Chuffs House and then turn right down Langworthy Lane. Walk all the way to the end of the lane and cross the road heading towards the byway opposite.

2 Continue along the byway, passing a concrete bollard and, at the end, turn left onto a lane, lined with pretty cottages. Soon pass a red-brick tower on your right and later pass the Belgian Arms pub on your left and then the duck pond.

There was a Prisoner of War camp at nearby Philiberts in the First World War. Apparently the pub used to be called the Eagle but had to change its name to stop the German POWs saluting it as they marched past!

3 Cross the road to reach the green, heading for the sundial of a cricketer and then bear right towards the George on the Green.

Cricket was played on the green until the 1960s when

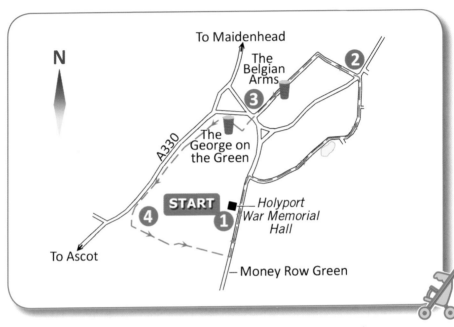

To Maidenhead

The Belgian Arms ❷

N

❸

A330

The George on the Green

START ■ ❶ —Holyport War Memorial Hall

❹

To Ascot

— Money Row Green

traffic got in the way. Apparently the cricket tea used to be served upstairs in the George on the Green. Both pubs used to be part of the Annual Beer Race, which was an important part of the Holyport Fair. Sadly, the beer race seems to have become a thing of the past but the fair still takes place every June.

Keep the pub on your left and skirt round it to pass a row of cottages with green doors. At the end of the cottages, continue straight ahead along a gravelly footpath and across a small bridge, with the busy Ascot Road to your right. Continue along this footpath until you reach a small lane.

❹ Turn left here (byway sign), passing magnificent gates with eagle gateposts on your right and then fields on your left. At a sign 'unsuitable for motor vehicles', go straight ahead down a path (restricted byway sign). Emerge on a lane and walk straight on, past houses, to reach a road. Turn left here to walk back along Money Row Green to return to the memorial hall.

Mapledurham

A wild wood and Toad Hall

Paved paths are a feature of this walk.

This lovely walk takes you through a golf course and then descends through Chazey Wood, with great views and the option of a visit to the splendid Mapledurham House. There is also a massive hill so this is not for the faint-hearted. A good workout, mainly on paved paths – which does make it easier to manage. Great blackberry-picking in season too.

Distance: 3¼ miles, with an optional extra 1½ mile (¾ mile each way) excursion to Mapledurham House.

Time: 1½ hours for main walk and allow an extra 40 minutes to go to Mapledurham House.

Terrain: Mainly paved bridleways and some grassy paths across a golf course, so if the weather is suitable for golf then you should be able to do this walk.

Start/Parking: The Pack Saddle pub, Chazey Heath, RG4 7UD. From Reading, head north through Caversham, along the A4074, for about 2 miles. You pass a golf course on your left and then you will see the Pack Saddle on your right. Park in the further car park. Please check with the landlord, though, before leaving your car in the pub car park.

OS map: Explorer 171 Chiltern Hills West or 159 Reading, Wokingham & Pangbourne; GR SU696771.

Refreshments: The Pack Saddle pub has a big garden, with a children's playground, plus highchairs and baby-changing facilities. ✆ 0118 946 3000.

Suggested picnic spot: None on this walk.

The Walk

❶ From the car park, head up the slope to the main road and cross with care to the lane opposite. After 50 metres, turn left along a byway, signposted to Caversham. Walk along this stony track with the golf course on either side, until you reach a track junction by Three Chimneys. Here, turn right along an asphalt path.

❷ This path descends gradually through tall trees and wild flowers into Chazey Wood. Pass Delta Force paintballing on your left and descend with views of fields ahead. The path bears left with fields on your right and a grain store ahead. Continue, passing the grain store and then at a T-junction turn left. You soon have excellent views of Mapledurham House on your right.

Mapledurham House is thought to have been E.H. Shepherd's inspiration for Toad Hall in his

illustrations of The Wind in the Willows. *The estate was bought by the Blount family in 1490 and has been owned by the same family ever since, although they lost it for a while after supporting the Royalists during the Civil War. Chazey Wood is part of the estate and another good bluebell spot during the season. Mapledurham Watermill* is the last working corn and grist mill on the Thames. It appeared in the Domesday Book and also in the 1976 film The Eagle Has Landed. *Mapledurham House is sometimes open to the public (see www.mapledurham.co.uk).*

❸ **Optional extra:** Here you have the option of walking to

Mapledurham House, an easy 1½ mile round trip along a paved bridleway. This section is flat and should take no more than 40 minutes. Or you may choose to admire from a distance. Either way, return to this point and walk back to the T-junction.

❹ Stay left to walk uphill (I did warn you!). Eventually, you reach the top of the hill and then another junction, where you turn right.

❺ Pass some farm buildings and then the paved path turns into a track and forks left, following the Chiltern Way up a grassy path with fields to your left and woods on your right.

Arrive at a cross-tracks, with a view of the golf clubhouse ahead. Turn right along a gravel track. After the track bends to the left, stay on the track (do not fork right) to go to the left of Hole 2.

❻ The track then dips down and back up to reach a waymark post. Follow a yellow arrow bearing left to walk along a grassy path next to a line of hawthorn bushes. Continue in this direction along the grassy path (the last 50 metres are annoyingly overgrown) to reach a T-junction. Turn left and walk back along the bridleway to reach a road. Turn right to reach the main road and cross it with care to return to the pub.

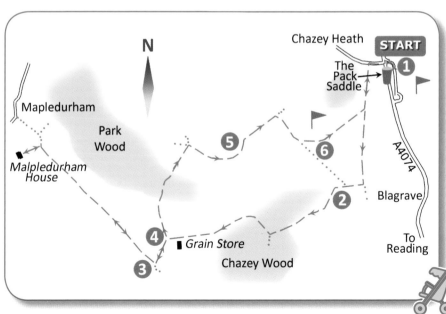

Jealott's Hill

A drover's walk

The 18th-century Cruchfield Manor House, passed along the way.

A **charming walk along country lanes** and bridleways, with wild
flowers along the route and a ford, plus surprisingly extensive views
from Jealott's Hill. There are bluebells in spring and blackberries and
sloes in autumn. Much of this walk is along old drover roads.

Distance: 4 miles.
Terrain: Lanes and stony tracks. Some of the tracks are quite arduous in places because of the number of small stones, but there is hardly any mud so this route is suitable all year round.
Start/Parking: Frost's Folly Country Car Park, Wellers Lane, Warfield. From the A3095 north of Bracknell, turn off eastwards at Moss End along Bowyer's Lane (opposite the Shepherd's House pub) and drive up to the top of the hill, where you bear right at a junction and then immediately turn left into Frost's Folly. Sat nav: RG42 6ER will take you to the Shepherd's House and then follow the directions above.
OS map: Explorer 160 Windsor, Weybridge & Bracknell; GR SU873726.
Refreshments: The Shepherd's House pub has a small garden and baby-changing facilities. ✆ 01344 423341. Moss End Garden Village – Warfield Village Café. ✆ 01344 483488. The café has booster seats and baby-changing facilities.
Suggested picnic spot: There are picnic tables at Frost's Folly and there is a bench by the ford at point 5 of the walk.

The Walk

1 From the car park, walk back through the main entrance, and turn right along the lane. Bear right at the triangle and walk along the lane. Pass Drown Boy Pond on your right and the entrance to the Syngenta Research Station on your left. Continue along the lane until you reach the A330, Ascot road.

2 Cross the A330 bearing slightly left to reach Snipes Lane opposite. Continue along Snipes Lane, which is a gravelly track. Pass through a gap next to a wooden gate and then turn left along an unmade road (this is Hawthorn Lane, a public byway).

Carpets of bluebells can be seen in the copse on your right in April/May.

3 After the copse, you will pass Lordlands Farm on your right and eventually the byway curves left to rejoin the main road.

Look out for Cruchfield Manor House to your right, by a large cedar.

4 Cross the A330 and immediately turn right along Hawthorndale Lane, a bridlepath. Continue along the

path as it weaves its way round the edge of the Research Station land, until you reach a junction where a permitted path forks right towards the A3095. There is a low wooden barrier to cross, which may be best done backwards with a pushchair.

5 Cross the A3095 to Pendrys Lane, opposite. Walk straight ahead along Pendrys Lane until you see a footbridge and ford ahead. Turn left just before the bridge, along a bridleway (Hazelwood Lane).

These bridleways are medieval drovers' roads, which were used to drive Berkshire pigs and sheep, as well as Somerset cattle and other livestock from further afield, all the way to Smithfield Market in London.

6 Walk along Hazelwood Lane, passing some caravans on your

The ford at point 5 of the route.

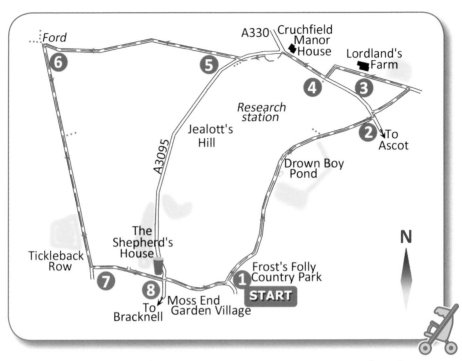

A330 Cruchfield
Manor
House

Lordland's
Farm

6 Ford

5

4

3

Research
station

Jealott's
Hill

A3095

2 To
Ascot

Drown Boy
Pond

The
Shepherd's
House

Tickleback
Row

7

8

Moss End
To Garden Village
Bracknell

Frost's Folly
Country Park

1 START

N

right and a byway (Gough's Barn Lane) on your left, and continue for ½ mile further until you reach a second bridleway on your left, which you take.

7 You soon pass a metal gate and continue past some houses to emerge onto a lane. Continue on until you reach the A3095, with the Shepherd's House pub on the left-hand corner. To reach Moss End Garden Village, turn right along the grass verge for 50 metres and then cross the road.

Legend has it that a local curate was found in a daze here after trying to

'investigate' a coven of witches. He subsequently had to leave the area. The New Leathern Bottle, just along the road, was also the subject of scandal in the 19th century, when it was run by a wife-beating landlord who eventually murdered his poor wife by throwing the marital bed on top of her.

8 From the Shepherd's House, cross the road and take the lane opposite, which goes gently uphill to reach a grassy triangle, at which you bear right to return to the car park.

Windsor Great Park

A perambulation

Enjoying the fallen leaves.

This wonderful walk takes place entirely within Windsor Great Park, former hunting ground of medieval kings and now a lovely mixture of parkland and forest. At times, though, you could be excused for thinking you were deep in the English countryside, walking along quiet country lanes with birds singing in the hedgerows and animals grazing in fields. Then every so often you catch sight of Windsor Castle and you wonder whether the Queen might chance to look out of her window to see you striding along with your buggy. Deer were reintroduced to the park about 30 years ago and often come close to the path, to the delight of little children.

Although the 6-mile route is one of the longest walks in the book, it is actually fairly easy since it is almost entirely on tarmac paths and so you don't get too much resistance when pushing your buggy. The Savill Garden café is halfway round and makes an excellent stop for feeding, changing and having a piece of cake with which to recharge your batteries.

Distance: 6 miles; short option: 2 miles.
Time: Allow 2½ hours plus stopping time; short option: allow 50 minutes.
Terrain: Almost entirely tarmac paths and the one sometimes muddy section can be avoided, so this walk is suitable all year round and in all conditions
Start/Parking: Cranbourne Gate free car park, SL4 2BT, on the A332 between Windsor and Ascot. Approaching from Windsor, take the A332 southwards. Pass the sign for Windsor Great Park and go up a hill to reach Cranbourne Gate car park on the right-hand side, opposite a pink house. **OS map:** Explorer 160 Windsor, Weybridge & Bracknell; GR SU947727.
Refreshments: About ½ mile from the start of the long or short walk, the Village Post Office and General Stores sells hot drinks, ice-creams and other refreshments and has outside tables, plus toilet facilities. ✆ 01753 865471. The excellent Savill Garden café, with its lovely cakes, is just what you need halfway round the walk. Highchairs are available, plus baby-changing facilities. ✆ 01784 435544.
Suggested picnic spot: By the Copper Horse statue overlooking the Long Walk in point 9 (note that this can easily be reached from the short walk by turning right for a short distance at point 10).

The Walk

. . . .

❶ From the car park, walk back to the main road and cross it. Go through the bridlegate by the pink house and straight ahead along the tarmac path, which sweeps round to the right and then downhill. Note that these roads are not open to general traffic but are used by workers on the estate so you may get the occasional car.

You soon have a superb view of

Windsor Castle to your left. This is the first of many!

❷ At the crossroads, turn right, following the sign towards the village and shop. At the next crossroads, turn left towards the village, bearing right at a fork, to keep a pond on your right. You soon reach the village shop on your left, where you can pause for a cup of tea. Continue along this path, passing the rest of the village on your left and then crossing a grassy tree-lined avenue, with a statue of a horse to your right and a millstone and the castle to your left. This is Queen Anne's Ride. Continue straight ahead, staying on the tarmac road, with glorious views on both sides.

❸ When you reach a crossroads, *either* **(short route)** turn left here and in 500 metres reach a crossroads with a gate to the deer park to your right. Turn left here and skip to point 10. **Or (long route)** continue straight ahead, going first downhill and then uphill into trees. As you go uphill you can see a bronze statue of a horse and rider to your left (the Copper Horse); you will be passing closer to this later on.

❹ The road sweeps up to the left and at the top you will pass Chaplain's Lodge on your right. Stay on the main tarmac path, ignoring paths to the right and following a wooden fence on your left. Shortly after a sandy bridleway (gallops) crosses your path, you reach a

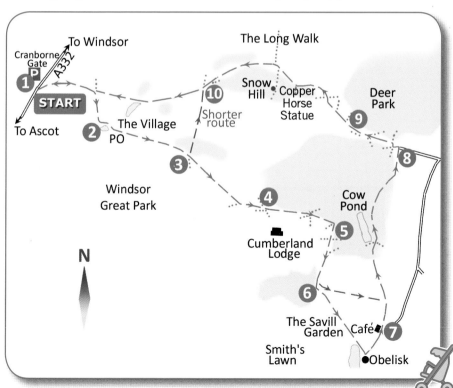

junction of four paths, with an oak grove in front of you. Take the second path on your right (not the first right towards Cumberland Lodge), so that you have nothing but oak trees on your left.

This oak grove was planted in 1937 to commemorate the Coronation of King George VI and Queen Elizabeth.

5 Continue on this path, past a sign saying 'children playing' and a few houses on your left, towards the polo ground.

This is Smith's Lawn and you can often see polo being played here during the summer. In the 1930s, Edward VIII used Smith's Lawn as an airfield when flying to and from his house, Fort Belvedere, which is on Shrubs Hill in the Great Park.

6 On reaching the polo ground at Cumberland Gate, you have a choice. **In good weather:** turn left along a wide grassy path, which leads up to the obelisk. At the obelisk, turn left to pass a refreshments kiosk on your left and a children's playground to your right. Bear left along the tarmac path to reach the Savill Garden shop and café on your left. **If it is muddy:** turn left along a tarmac path (just before the grassy path)

signposted to Savill Garden. This path turns left and then right and reaches the Savill Garden shop and café on your right.

The Long Walk leading to the castle.

Savill Garden is a beautiful ornamental garden with a mixture of woodland and formal gardens. There is a charge for entry but you can glimpse some of the garden while crossing the bridge over Obelisk Pond on your way up to the obelisk.

7 I'm going to assume that you at least pop into the Savill building to use the facilities but of course you can walk straight past if you want. Coming out of the Savill building, turn left along the tarmac path, following a sign towards the deer park. When the path veers left, take the stony/gravelly track straight ahead ('no cycling' sign) between rhododendron bushes. Continue along this track, ignoring cross-tracks and passing Cow Pond on your left. Eventually you pass a green gate and the path becomes tarmac. You soon reach a T-junction by a house and a sentry box.

8 Turn left and then immediately bear right along a bridleway (note that if this is muddy, you can continue straight ahead on the tarmac road and go right at the crossroads). Walk along this bridleway with the fence to the deer park on your right. When you reach the tarmac path, turn right and go through the gate into the park (press the button on the post to open the gates).

There are lots of semi-wild deer in this park and you would be unlucky not to see any. Older babies love them!

9 Stay on this tarmac path, which skirts around Snow Hill, eventually

passing the statue of the Copper Horse to your left.

This is a statue of George III dressed as a Roman emperor, riding a horse without stirrups, in the style of the Bronze horseman statue of Peter the Great in St Petersburg. Nearly three centuries before this was built, Henry VIII is supposed to have waited here for the sound of gunfire from the Round Tower, which signalled the execution of Anne Boleyn. The tree-lined avenue to your right is known as the Long Walk, which is 2.65 miles to Windsor Castle.

10 Eventually you reach a gate and exit the deer park (push the button on the post to open the gates). Continue straight ahead (the **short route** joins from your left). You can see the village ahead to your left. Pass the millstone and the village on your left. Then pass Prince Consort's Pond on your left. Ignore the first signpost and continue straight ahead to a second signpost and crossroads. At the crossroads, go straight on towards Cranbourne Gate, passing the 'closed to vehicles' sign and heading back uphill to the pink house where you started. When you reach Cranbourne Gate, cross the main road and return to the car park.

Dinton Pastures

A country park for all seasons

One of the many sculptures dotted around the park.

This country park is full of buggy-friendly footpaths and the walk I show here is simply one of a vast number of routes you could take. I have stuck to the better paths in order to create an all-year-round walk but do feel free to explore as you are unlikely to get your buggy stuck anywhere, although you may encounter a little mud. This is a dog walker's heaven so do not expect to feel 'away from it all' and it can get very busy at weekends. However, it is a great place to come with friends: both the paths and the café are able to cope with large numbers of pushchairs. There is a children's playground (including baby swings) near the start of the walk and lots of ducks to feed so you may want to bring some stale bread.

Distance: 2 miles.
Time: Allow 50 minutes.
Terrain: Tarmac paths and gravel tracks. Can get slightly muddy but is an all-year-round walk. This route is suitable for running.
Start/Parking: Dinton Pastures Country Park, RG10 0TH; entrance off Davis Street, the B3030 between Hurst, south of the A321, and the A329 at Winnersh. Park in the main car park (there is a charge).
OS map: Explorer 159 Reading; GR SU783719.
Refreshments: The Dragonfly Café at the park has both indoor and outdoor seating and also highchairs and baby-changing facilities.
✆ 0118 932 1071.
Suggested picnic spot: Lots of possibilities, including picnic tables by Black Swan Lake or by the café.

The Walk

1 From the car park, head towards the 'lakes, walks, play and picnic areas'. From the information sign, head along the main path, soon to cross a stream. Then fork left. Follow the hard surface path as it meanders around.

Dinton Pastures comprises 325 acres of park, including seven lakes and two rivers. The country park used to be the site of one of Berkshire's many gravel pits.

2 After passing a car park on your left-hand side and an information board on your right, turn right towards Black Swan Lake (ignore the sign to Tufty's Corner) and turn left along a wide gravel track alongside the lake.

Look out for the wooden sculptures of insects and snails etc, on your way round.

3 Stay on the gravel track as it bears left away from the lake, later passing the lake twice more and continuing straight ahead. At a fork in the path, head left towards White Swan Lake, crossing a small wooden bridge. At White Swan Lake, turn right along a gravel path. Stay on this main path, ignoring paths leading off either side and head into the trees.

4 At a T-junction, turn right to walk along Heron's Water. Eventually reach a T-junction and turn left towards Sandford Lake Conservation Area, with a stream on your left

The lakes are home to plenty of water birds.

and Sandford Lake on your right. When you reach an information board, with a road ahead of you, bear right, keeping the lake on your right-hand side. Keep going along this path until you cross a small wooden bridge and then turn left at a T-junction, with a signpost marked with a blue arrow and 'duck return'.

Sandford Mill can still be seen today (on the River Loddon, north-west of Sandford Lake), although it is now a private house. The mill was sacked and burned by Cromwell's

supporters during the Civil War but the current one was built in the 1770s and used until the 1950s.

5 Cross another bridge and soon pass Black Swan Sailing Club on your left. Continue straight ahead, keeping the lake on your right. When you reach a picnic area, usually full of ducks, bear left along a hard-surface path, passing a playground on your right. Bear left across a bridge to return to the car park. Note that the path off to your left leads straight to the café.

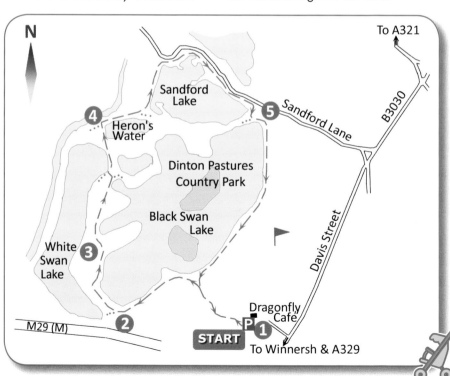

Swinley Forest and the Look Out

Forest tracks and heathland

Toddlers enjoying the swings.

Although the Look Out can get very busy, especially at weekends or in school holidays, Swinley Forest is big enough to accommodate a lot of people without feeling at all crowded. So, although you will pass dog walkers and cyclists, you will often feel as if you have the place to yourself. The forest tracks are excellent and you could even run this route if you are so inclined. There is a short option, as well as a shortcut on the longer route in case you need to hurry back to feed or change your baby. Older children will love the adventure playground at the Look Out.

Distance: 1½, 3 or 4 miles.
Time: 1¾ hours for the full route; 40 minutes if you take the shortcut in point 3; short option: 40 minutes.
Terrain: Forest tracks, which can be muddy after prolonged rainfall.
Start/Parking: The Look Out Discovery Centre (free parking), Nine Mile Ride, the B3430, just off the A322 at Bracknell. Follow the brown signs for the Look Out, RG12 7QW. OS map: Explorer 160 Windsor, Weybridge & Bracknell; GR SU878663.
Refreshments: The Look Out has a café and picnic tables outside, as well as a large adventure playground, which includes baby swings. Baby-changing facilities are also available.
Suggested picnic spot: At the Look Out.

The Walk

❶ From the Look Out Discovery Centre, follow signs to 'forest trails'. Go through a bridlegate, passing the 'Go Ape!' hut on your left, and walk through the trees along a wide track (with various tree-top activities either side of you). At a cross-tracks turn right. Continue to another cross-tracks and go straight ahead through a bridlegate. Head up the slope and at the top reach a cross-tracks with a gate on the left-hand side.

Swinley Forest was once part of Windsor Forest and is owned by the Crown Estate. There are a whopping 2,600 acres to explore, largely consisting of Scots pine woodland. The 'rides' through the forest were created for Queen Anne when she became too old to ride a horse, so

that she could hunt from the comfort of her carriage.

2 **For the short route:** continue straight ahead to reach a gate. Go through the gate and turn right along a wide track. After about 500 metres, another track joins from your left. Skip to the end of point 6. **For the long route:** turn left through the gate and go along the track. After 20 metres, cross over another track and at the next cross-tracks (with a red arrow pointing ahead) turn right.

3 A path soon joins from your left and you continue in this direction until you eventually reach a cross-tracks with dense pine trees on your left and bushes on your right. Turn right here and after 30 metres, cross over another track (*) and head straight on to reach Upper Star Post. **For a short cut:** turn right at the track (*) to head directly back to the Look Out; the way is signposted. This cuts approximately 1 mile off the full walk.

4 Follow the sign for 'Devil's Highway' ahead slightly left, along a wide track, lined with telegraph wires. (Note that although you are going to Caesar's Camp, the direct path is often full of very large puddles.) Follow this track for about 400 metres, until you reach a cross-tracks with another stony path.

Buggy Friendly Walks in The Thames Valley

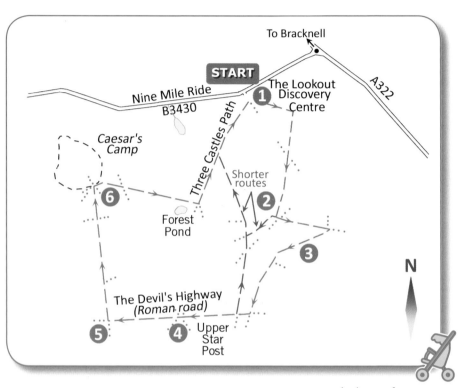

5 Turn right here and in about ½ mile you will reach another junction by the entrance to Caesar's Camp.

Caesar's Camp is an Iron Age hill fort built 700–500 BC, long before the Romans invaded. The whole thing was dug by hand using only basic tools and is supposed to resemble a giant oak leaf in shape. Annoyingly, the kissing-gate at the entrance is too small for buggies so you will have to admire from the

gate or carry your baby in if you want to take a look.

6 Take the track ahead signposted to the Look Out. This gravel path soon dips downhill, crossing another track. Shortly after passing Forest Pond on your right, reach a junction where you turn left, initially heading up a gentle slope. A track joins from your right (this is the **short route**). Continue in this direction to return to the Look Out, via the playground.

California Country Park

Along the boardwalk

The boardwalk over Longmoor Bog.

A **mixture of woods,** lake, ancient bogland and heathland. It is quiet here and there is a huge amount of wildlife, as well as interesting heathland where you may be lucky enough to see horses grazing. There is a children's playground (including baby swings) by the café and an enormous paddling pool, which is open in the summer.

The Walk

1 From the café, head towards the lake and turn right along the tarmac path, following the rhododendron bushes along the edge of the lake. Keep straight ahead at the cross-tracks, heading into trees. Soon turn left across a wooden bridge and then turn right along a tarmac path, which curves round to the left. At a fork, bear right but when the tarmac path leads towards a housing estate on your right, go straight on along a gravel track.

California Country Park was once park of Windsor Forest. In the 1920s, London coach parties were brought here on 'mystery tours'.

These became so popular that a proper holiday camp was set up and a ballroom was built with a floor made of coloured glass. During the Second World War, the ballroom remained an entertainment venue,

Distance: 2 miles.
Time: Allow 45 minutes.
Terrain: Tarmac paths, footpaths and wooden boardwalks. The route can get muddy in winter and the boardwalks slippery, although the walk around the lake will be fine in any weather.
Start/Parking: The café at California Country Park, RG40 4HT, reached from Nine Mile Ride, Finchampstead, just south of Wokingham. Take the A321 between Wokingham and Sandhurst. Approaching from Wokingham, bear right onto the B3016, then turn right onto Nine Mile Ride and look for the entrance to California Country Park on your right. Note that there is a charge for parking. **OS map:** Explorer 159 Reading; GR SU784651.
Refreshments: The California Dreaming Café, which has highchairs and baby-changing facilities. ✆ 0118 973 5519.
Suggested picnic spot: By the lake where there are picnic tables.

while the rest of the camp was used as a factory for aircraft parts.

❷ Keep going in this direction until you see another housing estate ahead and the path becomes tarmac again. At this point, turn left through the silver birch trees. Initially, keep left and follow the path through the woods. At a fork, go right and then fork left and turn left again along a more open path, with the woodland

Horses graze the heathland.

boundary to your right. Continue in this direction, eventually reaching a clearing with a caravan park in front of you. Bear right along a tarmac path between fences, which soon leads to rhododendron and holly bushes running alongside the lake.

3 When the path curves left, look out for a wooden gate to your right. Do not take this but 20 metres later, turn right down a track heading into trees. Soon, go through a wooden gate and head into heathland, with gorse bushes on either side.

4 Follow this obvious path round, to go through another gate and onto

the boardwalk.

This boardwalk takes you over the 8,000-year-old Longmoor Bog, which has been declared a Site of Special Scientific Interest, or SSSI, due to its 'abundance of rare sedges and mosses'.

5 You will soon see an orange stream to your right and then all around. At the end of the boardwalk, go through another gate and onto a gravel track. The path curves round and goes through another gate into pine trees. Eventually, you reach the lake again and bear right along the path to return to the café.